SUPER SPORTS STAR

BRETT FAVRE

Stew Thornley

Enslow Publishers, Inc.

40 Industrial Road   PO Box 38
Box 398   Aldershot
Berkeley Heights, NJ 07922 Hants GU12 6BP
USA   UK

http://www.enslow.com

Copyright © 2003 by Enslow Publishers, Inc.

Library of Congress Cataloging-in-Publication Data

Thornley, Stew.
   Super sports star Brett Favre / Stew Thornley.
      p. cm. — (Super sports star)
   Summary: Profiles the Green Bay Packers quarterback who has played in two Super Bowl games and is the only player to win or share the NFL Most Valuable Player Award in three consecutive years.
   Includes bibliographical references (p.) and index.
   ISBN 0-7660-2048-7
   1. Favre, Brett—Juvenile literature. 2. Football players—United States—Biography—Juvenile literature. [1. Favre, Brett. 2. Football players.] I. Title. II. Series.
   GV939.F29 T46 2003
   796.332'092—dc21   2002001722

Printed in the United States of America

10 9 8 7 6 5 4 3 2 1

To Our Readers:
We have done our best to make sure all Internet Addresses in this book were active and appropriate when we went to press. However, the author and the publisher have no control over and assume no liability for the material available on those Internet sites or on other Web sites they may link to. Any comments or suggestions can be sent by e-mail to comments@enslow.com or to the address on the back cover.

Photo Credits: © James Biever/NFL Photos, pp. 1, 22, 34; © Scott Boehm/NFL Photos, pp. 4, 15, 35; © Garrett Ellwood/NFL Photos, pp. 11, 18; © NFLP/JC Ridley/NFL Photos, pp. 13, 30; © NFLP/Joe Robbins/NFL Photos, pp. 16, 24, 26, 32; © Todd Rosenberg/NFL Photos, p. 20; © NFLP/Paul Spinelli/NFL Photos, p. 9; © David Stluka/NFL Photos, pp. 6, 37; © NFLP/David Stluka/NFL Photos, p. 42; © NFLP/Kevin Terrell/NFL Photos, pp. 7, 28, 39.

Cover Photo: © James Biever/NFL Photos.

CONTENTS

Introduction

Brett Favre is a quarterback. He plays for the Green Bay Packers in the National Football League (NFL).

A quarterback is usually the star player on a team. The quarterback hopes his offensive line will protect him. The offensive line is made up of players who protect the quarterback from the other team's defense. If the line breaks down, the quarterback may scramble. Quarterbacks try to avoid getting hit. They usually are not known as the toughest players in the league.

But Favre is different. He is tough. He has gotten hurt, but he has kept playing. Favre has started every game since early in the 1992 season.

Favre is a quarterback who plays like a linebacker. Linebackers are defensive players. They are always in the middle of the action, looking to hit and get hit.

A quarterback directs his team when it has the ball. The quarterback passes the ball to his receivers. Brett Favre can do that—but he can also do more. He may run with the ball himself. When he hands off to one of his running backs, he stays in the play. He may throw a block to help his runners get more yards. He plays quarterback like few others in the league.

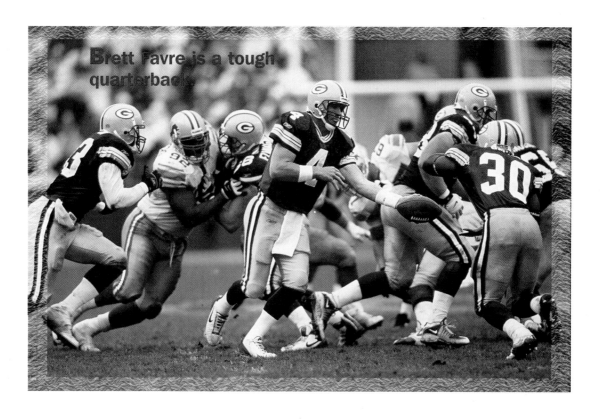

Brett Favre is a tough quarterback.

Winning the
Big One

The Green Bay Packers have won eleven NFL championships. That is more than any other team. The Packers also won the first two Super Bowls ever played in the 1960s. After that, the team did not do as well. The Packers lost more games than they won.

But in the early 1990s, they were getting better. A big reason was Brett Favre.

In 1996, the Packers won the National Football Conference (NFC) championship. This put them into the Super Bowl for the first time in nearly thirty years. Their opponents in the big game were the New England Patriots.

Brett Favre is usually confident. He believes in himself. But before the Super Bowl, Favre had the jitters. "I was real nervous," he said later. "As nervous as I'd been since fifth grade when I first played. I was scared I'd do something stupid or not be patient."

But Favre quickly got over it. On the second play of the game, he dropped back to pass. The Patriots put on a big pass rush—called a blitz.

On a blitz, more players than usual charge the quarterback. This means there are fewer players to cover the receivers. But if the defense can sack the quarterback, it does not matter.

Favre kept cool when the Patriots blitzed. He avoided the tacklers. He looked downfield and saw Andre Rison, one of his receivers. Favre threw a long pass, and it sailed into Rison's arms. Rison continued running, all the way to the end zone. It was good for a 54-yard touchdown. With the point after, Green Bay led, 7–0.

New England came back, though. The Patriots led, 14–10, in the second quarter, but Favre went

Brett Favre played his first Super Bowl against the New England Patriots in 1996.

to work again. This time he hit Antonio Freeman with a long pass. It turned into an 81-yard touchdown play. It was the longest pass in Super Bowl history. The play put the Packers back in the lead.

Favre was still not done. He later ran for a touchdown. The Packers beat the Patriots, 35–21.

"I love football," Favre once said. "My favorite moment is right after I throw a touchdown. The crowd roars. I am on top of the world."

Thanks to Favre, so were the Green Bay Packers.

★★★ UP CLOSE

Brett Favre's favorite football players as a kid were, Archie Manning and Roger Staubach.

Growing Up
Near the Gulf

CHAPTER 2

11

Brett Favre grew up near the Gulf of Mexico. He was born on October 10, 1969, in Gulfport, Mississippi, to Irvin and Bonita Favre. The Favre family lived a few miles north, just outside the small town of Kiln, Mississippi. The town's name is said "Kill." The name Favre is also said differently than it is spelled. It is pronounced "Farve."

Brett Favre played in different sports when he was younger. He had a strong throwing arm. Once, in a basketball game, Favre threw a long pass. It sailed the length of the court and struck a fire extinguisher on the wall. It hit so hard that the fire extinguisher fell off the wall and broke. Favre was only in fifth grade at the time.

Favre's strong arm helped him in baseball. He played third base, and he had no trouble making the long throw across the diamond. Brett played baseball five years for the Hancock North Central High School baseball team. His father was the coach. Brett was the best player on the team.

When Brett Favre
was a kid, he played
many sports.

But Favre was even better in football. He played for his father in high school football, too, and he could play many positions. On defense, he played safety, a defensive back who covers the other team's receivers. Favre also punted and did the place kicking for the team. But his best position was on offense. Favre was the quarterback. Once again, his powerful right arm came in handy.

Favre was one of the best quarterbacks in the state. He played in the Mississippi high school all-star game after his senior season. Great high school players sometimes get offers for a college scholarship. If they play for the college's team, their education and books are paid for.

Only some college recruiters had their eyes on Favre. The North Central High School team ran the ball a lot on offense. It worked, but it did not show how well Favre could throw the ball.

Because of that, Favre did not get too many college offers. He was leaning toward playing at

Delta State, a small college in Cleveland, Mississippi. He also thought about going to Pearl River Junior College. But then the University of Southern Mississippi offered him a scholarship.

Southern Mississippi was a larger school. Favre's father had played baseball there. His older brother, Scott, had been quarterback on the football team. Favre planned to go to Southern Mississippi and play for the Golden Eagles, just like his father and brother.

Brett Favre gets ready to throw the ball.

CHAPTER 3

Larger Than Life

In 1987, Brett Favre was to play on defense for Southern Mississippi. The team already had a number of good quarterbacks. But Favre wanted to show them he was a good quarterback, too.

He quickly got his chance. In Southern Mississippi's second game of Favre's first season, the Golden Eagles were losing to the Tulane Green Wave. They needed to try something different if they were going to win. In the third quarter, Favre went in as quarterback.

He threw two touchdown passes. Thanks to Favre, Southern Mississippi came back to win the game. The next day, coach Jim Carmody said that Favre would be the team's starting quarterback. Favre set a school record that year by throwing fifteen passes for touchdowns. It was a great start. There were a few problems, though. Too many of Favre's passes were not caught, or incomplete. Even worse, thirteen of them had been intercepted.

Favre knew he would have to get better, and he did. In 1988, he completed more than half the passes he threw. He racked up 2,271 yards in passing—a school record. He also broke his own touchdown record by connecting for sixteen scores. That season he had only five interceptions. With Favre in charge, the Golden Eagles had a record of ten wins and two losses. Favre did well because he believed in himself. His teammates believed in him, too. Jeff Bower, the team's offensive coordinator, thought Favre's confidence was a big reason the team

In 1988, Favre set a University of Southern Mississippi record with 2,271 yards in passing.

did so well. "When you have that kind of an attitude," Bower said, "it rubs off on other guys."

Favre continued to get better. When he was a junior, Southern Mississippi played Florida State University, a powerful team. Favre passed for 282 yards. Two of those passes were good for touchdowns. The Golden Eagles beat Florida State, 30–24. It was a great victory. "Brett just might be as good as any quarterback around," said Curley Hallman, who was now the coach at Southern Mississippi.

As Favre went into his senior season, some thought he might be able to win the Heisman Trophy. The Heisman Trophy is the greatest award in college football. It goes to the best player of the year.

In the summer of 1990, Favre was in a car accident. He was badly hurt. He got out of the hospital and went back to school. But he still was not feeling well. He went back to the hospital. After surgery, he was well again.

It looked like Favre might miss his whole senior season. Fortunately, he was back in a few weeks. In his first game, he led Southern Mississippi to a win against the Alabama Crimson Tide. Gene Stallings, Alabama's coach, was impressed. "You can call it a miracle or a legend or whatever you want to," he said of

Brett Favre had a great college football career. He was now ready to go on.

Favre. "I just know that on that day, Brett Favre was larger than life."

Even though he missed the first part of the year, Favre led the Golden Eagles to a record of 8–4. He played in a couple of all-star games after the season, including the East-West Shrine game.

Favre had set a lot of career passing records at Southern Mississippi. He did great things in his college career. Now he was ready to do even more.

★★★ UP CLOSE

Playing sports seems to run in the Favre family. Brett Favre's older brother Scott was quarterback for Mississippi State. His younger brother, Jeff, was a free safety on the Southern Mississippi football team.

Comeback Kid

Favre missed several games his senior season after the car accident. Because of that, a lot of professional teams did not want to pick Favre in the NFL draft. The NFL draft is the way that professional football teams pick new players each year.

One person who was interested in Favre was Ron Wolf, general manager of the New York Jets. He made the decisions on which players to draft. The Jets had the thirty-fourth pick in the draft. Wolf was hoping Favre would still be available. But the Atlanta Falcons had the thirty-third pick, right before the Jets. The Falcons drafted Favre. Wolf was upset, but he did not forget Favre.

But, it seemed like the Falcons forgot about Favre. They already had a quarterback, Chris Miller. Favre was a backup to Miller, and he barely played in 1991. After the season, the

Falcons decided to trade Favre to another team. By this time, Ron Wolf was the general manager of the Green Bay Packers. Wolf had missed getting Favre a year before, but this time he got his man. Wolf worked out a trade with the Falcons, and Favre became a Green Bay Packer.

Brett Favre shows his concentration as he looks for an open receiver.

Favre would still be a backup. The Packers had Don Majkowski, a very good quarterback. The Packers lost their first two games of the 1992 season. Then, early in their third game, Majkowski got hurt. In came Favre. The Packers fell behind to the Cincinnati Bengals. Favre led a fourth-quarter comeback.

Green Bay trailed, 23–17, late in the fourth quarter. The Packers were on their own 8-yard line, a long way from the other end zone. Favre got them closer with a 42-yard pass to Sterling Sharpe. The Packers gained some more yards. They were at the Bengals' 35-yard line. There were under thirty seconds left to play. Favre let loose with a long pass for Kitrick Taylor. He then shut his eyes. "I was scared I had thrown it halfway up in the seats," he said. "I closed my eyes and listened for the cheers and when I heard them, I knew we either scored or were close." The Packers had scored. After Chris Jacke kicked the extra point, Green Bay had a 24–23 win.

Brett Favre has played in several Pro Bowls.

Majkowski's injury was not serious. The Packers thought they would put him back in the lineup when he got better. But Favre made the most of his chance to fill in. He did so well that he kept the starting job even after Majkowski got better.

With Favre as quarterback, Green Bay finished in second place in their Division and almost made the playoffs. Favre played in the Pro Bowl, the NFL all-star game. In 1993, the Packers got to the playoffs for the first time since 1982. Once again, Favre made the Pro Bowl.

Brett Favre had come back from a lot and was one of the best in the game. But others knew he could do even better. It was up to Favre to see that, too.

CHAPTER 5

Getting Serious About the Game

Even though Favre was doing well, he did not focus on football as much as he should have. He was getting by on his football skills. He often chose having a good time instead of working hard.

His coaches and others knew what would happen if he got serious. There would be no stopping him. Finally, Favre figured this out for himself.

He spent more time watching game films. He went to his coaches for advice. He studied his playbook instead of going to parties. "I applied myself like never before," Favre said.

In 1994, Favre completed more than 60 percent of his passes. He connected for thirty-three touchdowns. And his interception total dropped from twenty-four to fourteen.

The Packers won their last three games of the season to make the playoffs. They beat the Detroit Lions in the first round. They then lost to the Dallas Cowboys, who went on to win the Super Bowl.

In 1995, the Packers made it even further. They finished with a record of eleven wins and five losses. That was the best in the NFC Central Division. It was the first time the Packers won their division since 1972. And Favre was the best player in the entire league.

His passing totals soared. In one game, he completed a 99-yard touchdown pass to Robert Brooks. Favre led the NFL in passing yards and in

Brett Favre has worked very hard to be a great football player.

touchdown passes, and his number of interceptions dropped again.

"He does everything you can ask from a quarterback, and he's still young and learning," said his coach, Mike Holmgren. The Packers went to the NFC championship game, only a step away from the Super Bowl. But they lost to Dallas again.

Even so, Favre was named the Most Valuable Player (MVP) in the NFL. "It means everything," Favre said of the honor. "It's the National Football League, which means it's the best player in the world. And that's awesome."

Favre also made a promise to the Green Bay fans. He told them the Packers would win the Super Bowl in 1996.

Favre had another problem to deal with, though. He often played when he was hurt. To do that, he took painkillers. He became addicted. In May 1996, Favre went through treatment. He kicked the addiction. Although he is a tough player, overcoming his addiction

In 1996, Brett Favre promised Green Bay fans that the Packers would make it to the Super Bowl.

was one of the toughest things he ever had to do.

Favre then kept his promise to the fans. In the season opener, he threw four touchdown passes. He had three each in the next two games. The Packers won their first three games before losing to the Minnesota Vikings. Then they came back with five straight wins. The Packers had not won that many games in a row since 1966. That was the year the team won its first Super Bowl.

Green Bay finished the regular season with a record of thirteen wins and three losses. That was the best in the NFC and tied for the best in the entire NFL.

The Packers beat the San Francisco 49ers in the first playoff game. The next game was against the Carolina Panthers for the NFC championship. The Packers had made it this far the year before but were then beaten. There was no stopping them this time. Carolina took a 7–0 lead, but Green Bay tied it after a 29-yard touchdown pass from Favre to Dorsey Levens. A field goal put Carolina back in front, but the Packers came back. Favre hit Antonio Freeman with a pass for a touchdown, which put Green Bay ahead.

The Packers beat Carolina, 30–13, and made it to the Super Bowl. The New England Patriots were no match for Green Bay in the big game. The Packers won, 35–21.

For the second year in a row, Favre was the MVP of the NFL. Winning the MVP is great. But this year Favre had something even better. It was a Super Bowl championship.

In 1996, the Packers won the Super Bowl.

Another Super Year

Winning the Super Bowl is a tough act to follow. But Favre and the Packers had another great season in 1997. Favre led the league with thirty-five touchdown passes. Five of those came in one game against the Minnesota Vikings in September. The Vikings were ahead, 7–0. But Favre led the Packers back. He threw to Robert Brooks for a 19-yard touchdown to tie the game. Then he connected with Antonio Freeman. The 28-yard touchdown pass put the Packers ahead. A few minutes later, Favre and Freeman teamed up for another touchdown. Favre then threw a laser to Terry Mickens for a touchdown late in the second quarter. Favre added another touchdown pass in the second half. Green Bay won the game, 38–24.

Favre's big day against the Vikings gave him 156 touchdown passes for his career. That broke the Packers team record, which had been held by Bart Starr.

Green Bay won its final five games of the

Brett Favre has been playing for the Green Bay Packers since 1992.

regular season. The Packers finished with a record of 13–3, the same as the year before. They also made it back to the Super Bowl. This time, though, they did not do as well. They played the Denver Broncos in a close and exciting game. But Denver scored a touchdown late in the game to break a tie. The Broncos won the game, 31–24.

Favre had another great season. He and Barry Sanders of the Detroit Lions were named the Most Valuable Players of the NFL. It was the third straight year that Favre won or shared the MVP award. No player had ever done that before.

The Packers made the playoffs again in 1998. They played the San Francisco 49ers in the first round. With Green Bay trailing in the fourth quarter, Favre led the Packers on an 89-yard touchdown drive to put them ahead. But San Francisco came back and scored with three seconds left to win. The Packers were knocked out of the playoffs.

The Packers have not done as well in the years since then. But Favre has continued to be a steady performer in Green Bay.

He has also settled down in his life off the field. He and his wife, Deanna, have a home in Hattiesburg, Mississippi. Hattiesburg is where Favre went to college. It is also not far from Kiln, where he and Deanna grew up. Brett and Deanna have a daughter, Brittany, who was born in 1989. Another daughter, Breleigh, was born in 1999.

Brett Favre has been in a movie and several commercials.

Favre gets excited about football. But he gets even more excited when he talks about his family. "I want to be there," he said of his daughter, Breleigh. "I want to be the first person she sees when she wakes up and the last person she sees when she goes to sleep."

★ UP CLOSE

Brett Favre started the Brett Favre Forward Foundation. The Foundation donates money to charities in Mississippi and Wisconsin.

CAREER STATISTICS

NFL									
Passing									
Year	Team	GP	Comp.	Att.	Yds.	Pct.	TDs	Int.	Rating
1991	Atlanta	2	0	5	0	0.0	0	2	0.0
1992	Green Bay	15	302	471	3,227	64.1	18	13	85.3
1993	Green Bay	16	318	522	3,303	60.9	19	24	72.2
1994	Green Bay	16	363	582	3,882	62.4	33	14	90.7
1995	Green Bay	16	359	570	4,413	63.0	38	13	99.5
1996	Green Bay	16	325	543	3,899	59.9	39	13	95.8
1997	Green Bay	16	304	513	3,867	59.3	35	16	92.6
1998	Green Bay	16	347	551	4,212	63.0	31	23	87.8
1999	Green Bay	16	341	595	4,091	57.3	22	23	74.7
2000	Green Bay	16	338	580	3,812	58.3	20	16	78.0
2001	Green Bay	16	314	510	3,921	61.6	32	15	94.1
Totals		**161**	**3,311**	**5,442**	**38,627**	**60.8**	**287**	**172**	**86.8**

CAREER STATISTICS

NFL						
Rushing						
Year	Team	GP	Att.	Yds.	Avg.	TDs
1991	Atlanta	2	0	0	0	0
1992	Green Bay	15	47	198	4.2	1
1993	Green Bay	16	58	216	3.7	1
1994	Green Bay	16	42	202	4.8	2
1995	Green Bay	16	39	181	4.6	3
1996	Green Bay	16	49	136	2.8	2
1997	Green Bay	16	58	187	3.2	1
1998	Green Bay	16	40	133	3.3	1
1999	Green Bay	16	28	142	5.1	0
2000	Green Bay	16	27	108	4.0	0
2001	Green Bay	16	38	56	1.5	1
Totals		161	426	1,559	3.7	12

GP—Games Played
GS—Games Started
Att.—Passes Attempted

Comp.—Passes Completed
Pct.—Percentage of Passes Completed
Yds.—Yards Passing

TDs—Touchdown Passes
Int.—Interceptions
No.—Number of carries

Where to Write to Brett Favre

Mr. Brett Favre
c/o Green Bay Packers
1265 Lombardi Avenue
Green Bay, Wisconsin 54304

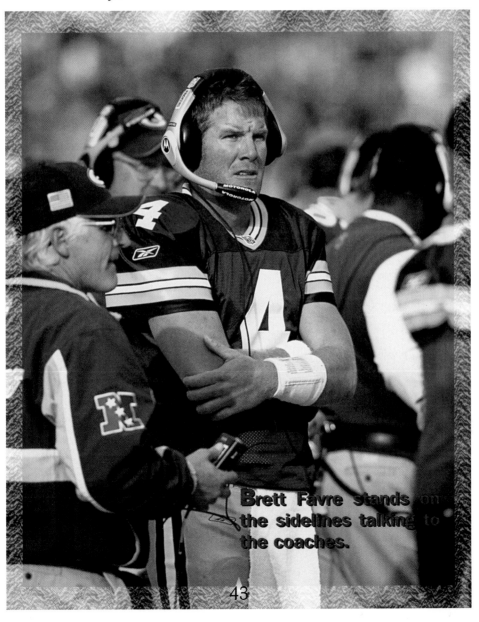

Brett Favre stands on the sidelines talking to the coaches.

WORDS TO KNOW

blitz—A play where the defense rushes with more than its linemen. Linebackers and defensive backs may rush the quarterback on the blitz.

cornerback—A defensive back. It is his job to cover receivers.

draft—A selection of players by teams, who take turns choosing the players they want.

fullback—The fullback is normally called upon whenever short yardage is needed. He is usually the most powerful runner on the team. He can drive straight ahead into the line or block for other runners.

Heisman Trophy—The award that is given each year to the best college football player in America.

line of scrimmage—The place that the play starts on the field.

nose guard—A defensive player who usually lines up over center.

quarterback—He is in charge of the offense. He calls the plays, sometimes with help from the bench. The quarterback can either pass the ball, hand it off to a running back, or keep it and run.

rookie—A player in his first full season in professional sports.

sack—To tackle a quarterback attempting to pass the ball behind the line of scrimmage.

safety—Another defensive back who covers receivers, like a cornerback. A safety is also a play when the defense tackles a player in his own end zone. The defensive team gets two points if it gets a safety.

secondary—If a runner gets past the line of scrimmage, he has to get past the players in the secondary further downfield.

tailback—A quick runner who is usually lighter and faster than the fullback. He most often slashes through openings in the line or runs outside, and for longer yardage.

tight end—Usually a big player who catches passes and blocks for runners.

READING ABOUT

Books

Dougherty, Terri. *Brett Favre.* Minneapolis, Minn.: ABDO Publishing Co., 1999.

Molzahn, Arlene Bourgeois. *The Green Bay Packers Football Team.* Berkeley Heights, N.J.: Enslow Publishers, Inc., 1999.

Potts, Steve. *Green Bay Packers*. North Mankato, Minn.: Smart Apple Media, 2001.

Stewart, Mark. *Brett Favre: Leader of the Pack.* Danbury, Conn.: Children's Press, 1999.

Internet Addresses

The Official Web Site of the NFL
<http://www.nfl.com>

The Official Web Site of the Packers
<http://www.packers.com/team/players/favre_brett/index.html>

INDEX